Impressum
Verlag: BABADADA GmbH, Nedderfeld 112 , 22529 Hamburg
Geschäftsführer / Verlagsleitung: Harald Hof
Druck: Books on Demand GmbH, In de Tarpen 42, 22848 Norderstedt

Imprint
Publisher: BABADADA GmbH, Nedderfeld 112 , 22529 Hamburg, Germany
Managing Director / Publishing direction: Harald Hof
Print: Books on Demand GmbH, In de Tarpen 42, 22848 Norderstedt, Germany

School
škola

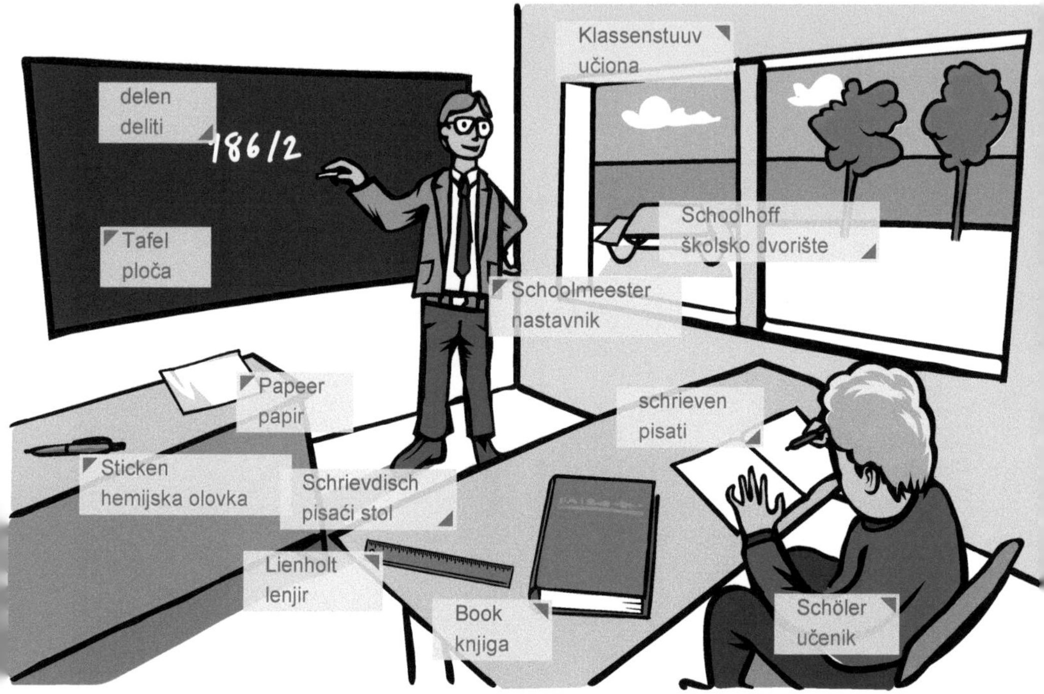

Klassenstuuv
učiona
delen
deliti
186/2
Tafel
ploča
Schoolhoff
školsko dvorište
Schoolmeester
nastavnik
Papeer
papir
schrieven
pisati
Sticken
hemijska olovka
Schrievdisch
pisaći stol
Lienholt
lenjir
Book
knjiga
Schöler
učenik

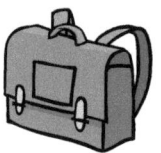

Ranzel

torba

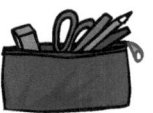

Feddermapp

pernica

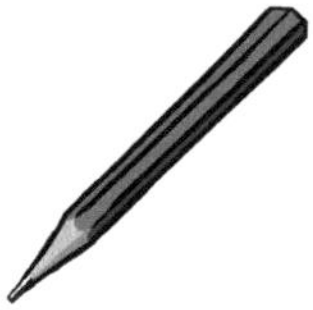

Bleesticken

grafitna olovka

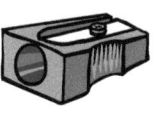

Scharpmaker

šiljilo za olovke

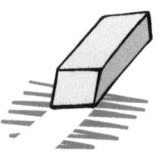

Radeergummi

gumica za brisanje

Tekenblock

blok za crtanje

Teken
crtež

Pinsel
kist

Malkassen
kutija sa bojama

Scheer
makaze

Klever
lepilo

Heft to'n Öven
beležnica

Huusopgaav
domaći zadatak

Tall
broj

tohooptellen
sabirati

aftrecken
oduzimati

malnehmen
množiti

reken
računati

Bookstaav
slovo

ABC
abeceda

hello

Woort
reč

Text

tekst

lesen

čitati

Kried

kreda

Stunn

čas

Klassenbook

dnevnik

Pröven

ispit

Tüügnis

svedočanstvo

Schooluniform

školska uniforma

Utbillen

obrazovanje

Nakieksel

leksikon

Universität

univerzitet

Mikroskop

mikroskop

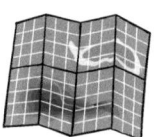

Koort

karta

Papeerkorf

košara za papir

Hotel
hotel

Grand

Harbarg
prenoćište

ROOMS

Wesselstuuv
menjačnica

EXCHANGE

D

Kuffer
kofer

Auto
auto

Spraak

jezik

jo / ne

da / ne

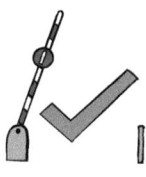

Jo

okej

Moin

zdravo

Översetter

prevodilac

Dank ok

hvala

Wat kost...?

Koliko košta...?

Ik verstah nich

ne razumem

Problem

problem

Goden Avend

dobro veče!

Moin!

Dobro jutro!

Gode Nacht!

Laku noć!

Tschüüs

doviđenja

Richt

smer

Bagaasch

prtljaga

Tasch

torba

Rüchsack

ruksak

Gast

gost

Stuuv

soba

Slaapsack

vreća za spavanje

Telt

šator

Touristeninformatschoon

turističke informacije

Strand

plaža

Kreditkoort

kreditna kartica

Fröhstück

doručak

Meddageten

ručak

Avendeten

večera

Fohrkort

karta za vožnju

Fohrstohl

lift

Breefmark

poštanska markica

Grenz

granica

Toll

carina

Bottschop

ambasada

Visum

viza

Pass

pasoš

Transport

transport

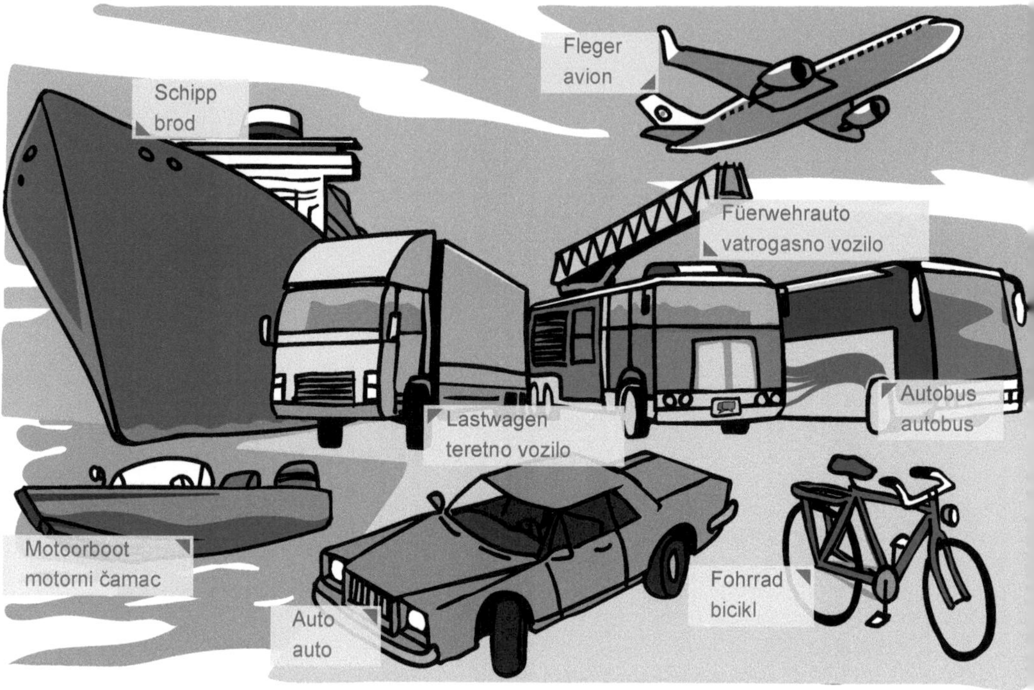

Fleger
avion
Schipp
brod
Füerwehrauto
vatrogasno vozilo
Autobus
autobus
Lastwagen
teretno vozilo
Motoorboot
motorni čamac
Fohrrad
bicikl
Auto
auto

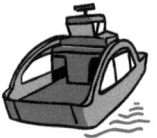

Fähr

trajekt

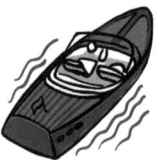

Boot

čamac

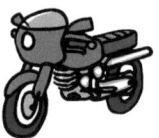

Motoorrad

motocikl

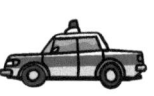

Polizeiauto

policijski auto

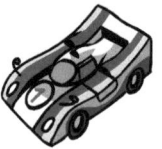

Rönnauto

trkaći auto

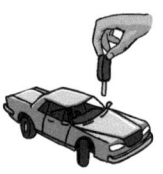

Lehnwagen

iznajmljeno auto

Carsharing

delenje automobila

Afsleepwagen

vučno vozilo

Müllauto

vozilo za odvoz smeća

Motoor

motor

Kraftstoff

benzin

Tanksteed

benzinska stanica

Verkehrsschild

saobraćajni znak

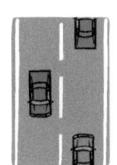

Verkehr

saobraćaj

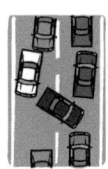

Stau

zastoj

Afstellplatz

parkiralište

Bahnhoff

železnička stanica

Sporen

šine

Tog

voz

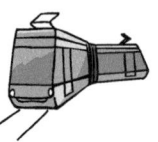

Stratenbahn

tramvaj

Wagon

vagon

Dwarsmöhl

helikopter

Flooghaven

aerodrom

Tower

kula

Fohrgast

putnik

Grootkist

kontejner

Karton

karton

Koor

kolica

Korf

korpa

starten / lannen

uzleteti / sleteti

Stadt

grad

Dörp

selo

Binnenstadt

centar grada

Huus

kuća

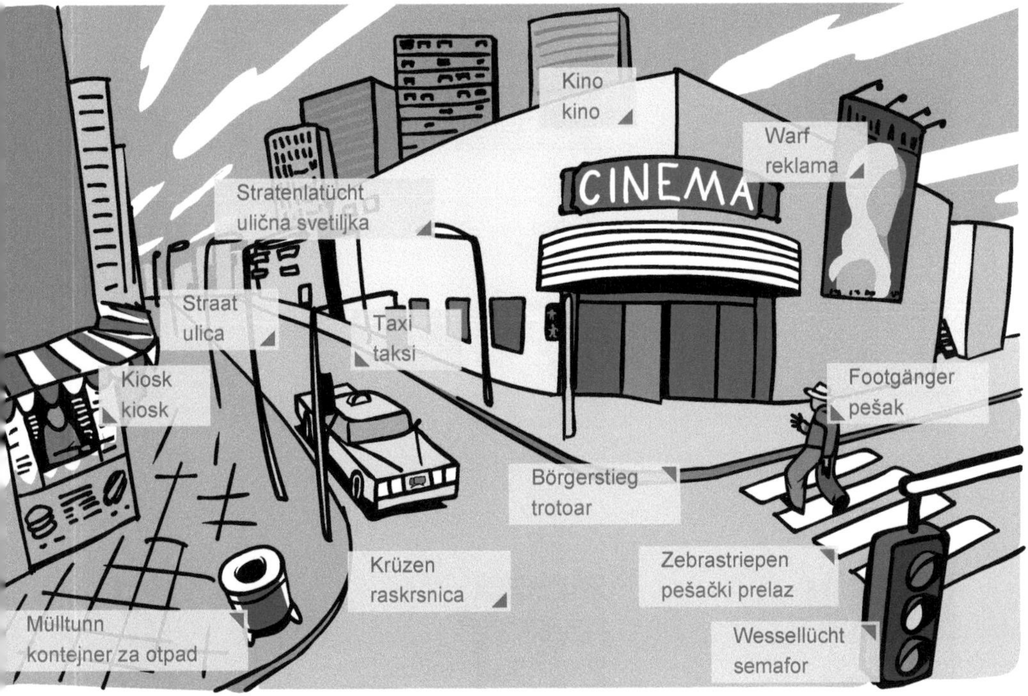

Kino
kino

Warf
reklama

Stratenlatücht
ulična svetiljka

CINEMA

Straat
ulica

Taxi
taksi

Footgänger
pešak

Kiosk
kiosk

Börgerstieg
trotoar

Krüzen
raskrsnica

Zebrastriepen
pešački prelaz

Mülltunn
kontejner za otpad

Wessellücht
semafor

Hütt
....
koliba

Wahnung
....
stan

Bahnhoff
....
železnička stanica

Raathuus
....
većnica

Museum
....
muzej

School
....
škola

Universität
univerzitet

Bank
banka

Krankenhuus
bolnica

Hotel
hotel

Afteek
apoteka

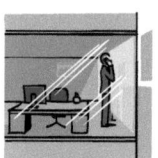

Büro
kancelarija

Bookhökerie
knjižara

Hökerie
prodavnica

Blomenhökerie
cvećara

Supermarkt
supermarket

Markt
trg

Koophuus
robna kuća

Fischhökerie
ribarnica

Inkoopszentrum
trgovački centar

Haven
luka

Parkanlaag

park

Bank

klupa

Brüch

most

Trepp

stepenice

Ünnergrundbahn

podzemna željeznica

Tunnel

tunel

Busstoppsteed

autobuska stanica

Bar

bar

Spieslokal

restoran

Breefkassen

poštansko sanduče

Stratenschild

ulični znak

Parkklock

parkirni automat

Deertenpark

zoološki vrt

Baadanstalt

bazen

Moschee

džamija

Buernhoff

seosko gazdinstvo

Ümweltversmudden

zagađenje okoline

Karkhoff

groblje

Kark

crkva

Speelplatz

igralište

Tempel

hram

Landschop
pejsaž

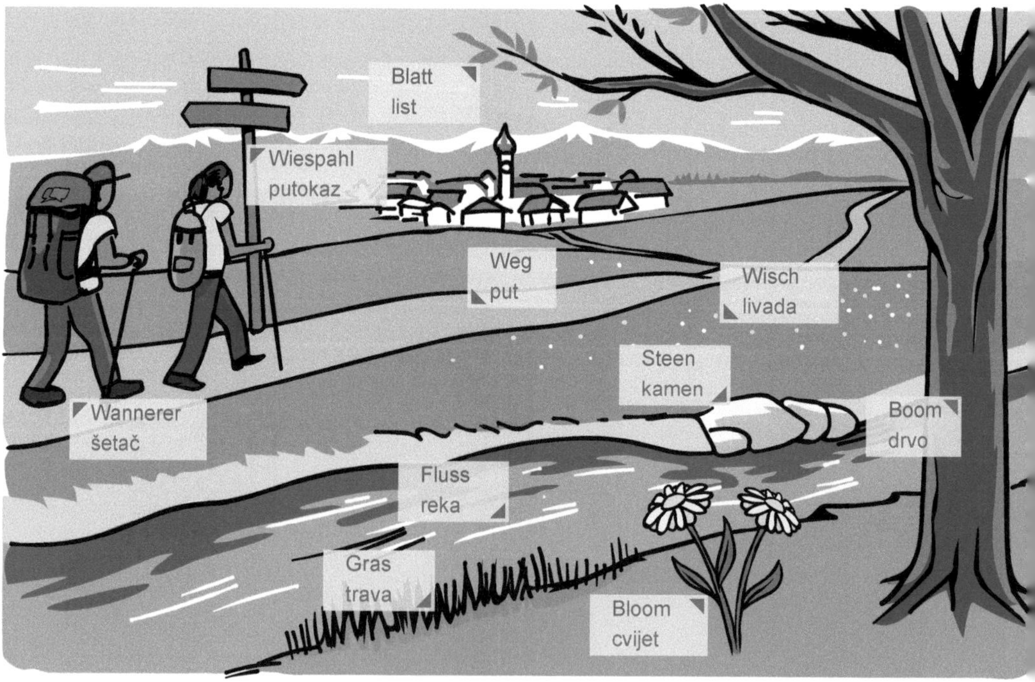

Blatt
list

Wiespahl
putokaz

Weg
put

Wisch
livada

Steen
kamen

Wannerer
šetač

Boom
drvo

Fluss
reka

Gras
trava

Bloom
cvijet

Daal

dolina

Barg

planina

See

jezero

Holt

šuma

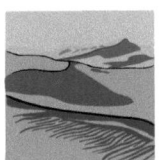

Wööst

pustinja

Füerspien Barg

vulkan

Slott

dvorac

Regenbagen

duga

Poggenstohl

gljiva

Palm

palma

Steekmück

moskito

Fleeg

muva

Miegeemk

mrav

Imm

pčela

Spinn

pauk

Sebber

buba

Pogg

žaba

Katteker

veverica

Swienegel

jež

Haas

zec

Uul

sova

Vagel

ptica

Swaan

labud

Wildswien

divlja svinja

Hirsch

jelen

Elk

los

Staudamm

nasip

Windrad

vetrenjača

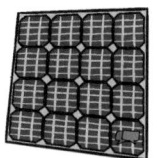

Solarmodul

solarna ploča

Klima

klima

Spieslokal
restoran

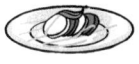

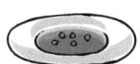

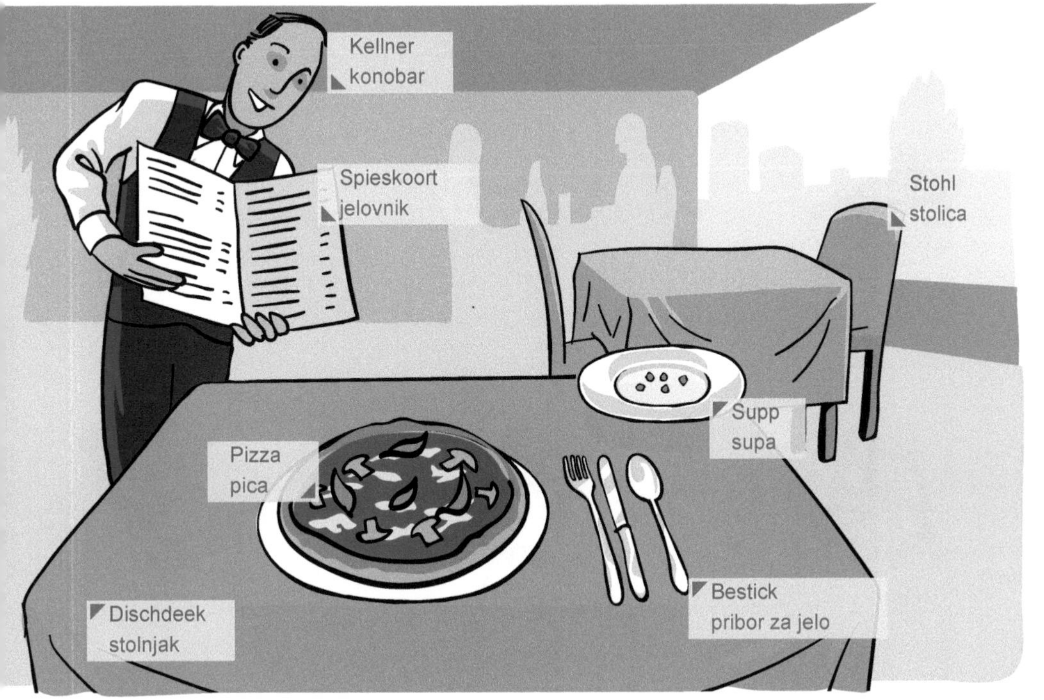

Kellner
konobar
Spieskoort
jelovnik
Stohl
stolica
Supp
supa
Pizza
pica
Dischdeek
stolnjak
Bestick
pribor za jelo

Vörspies
predjelo

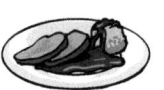

Haupteten
glavno jelo

Nadisch
desert

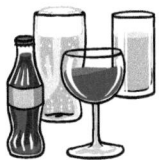

Drünk
napitci

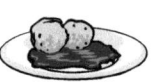

Eten
jelo

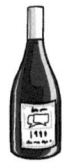

Buddel
flaša

Fastfood

brza hrana

Strateneten

imbis hrana

Teekann

čajnik

Zuckerdoos

doza za šećer

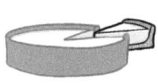

Portschoon

porcija

Espressomaschien

aparat za espresso

Hoochstohl

visoka stolica

Reken

račun

Tablett

poslužavnik

Mess

nož

Gavel

viljuška

Lepel

kašika

Teelepel

čajna kašika

Munddook

salveta

Glas

čaša

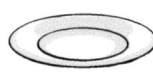

Töller

tanjir

Suppentöller

tanjir za supu

Ünnertass

tanjirić

Sooß

sos

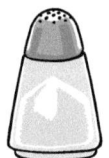

Soltstreuer

soljenka

Pepermöhl

mlin za biber

Etig

sirće

Ööl

ulje

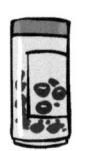

Krüder

začini

Ketchup

kečap

Mostrich

senf

Mayonnaise

majoneza

Supermarkt
supermarket

Anbott
ponuda
FOR
Kunn
kupac
Melkprodukten
mlečni proizvodi
Aaft
voće
Inkoopswagen
kolica za kupovinu

BUTCHERS

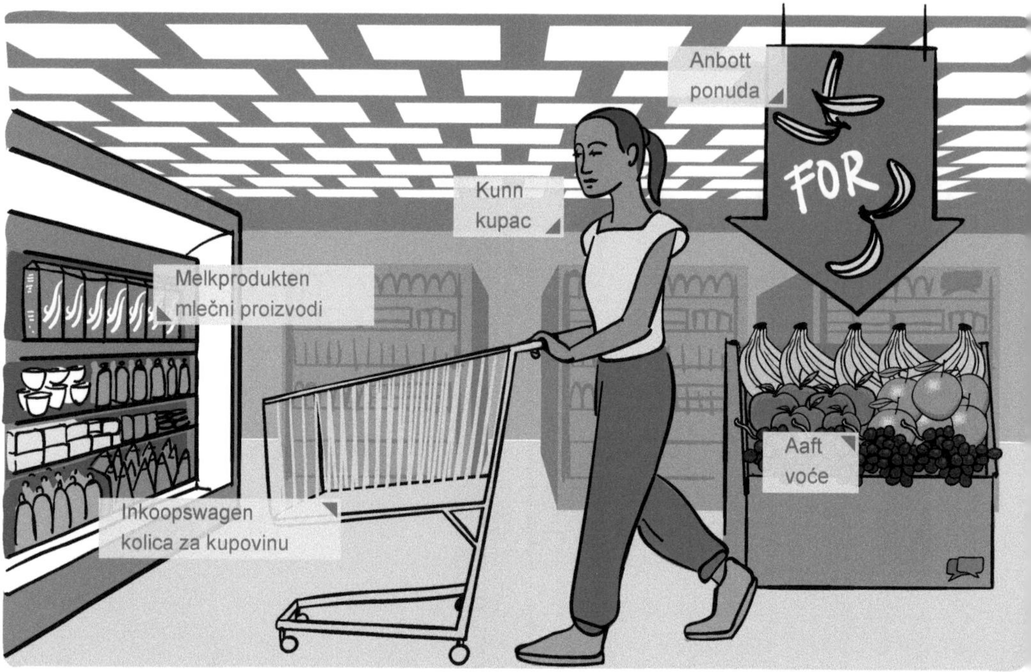

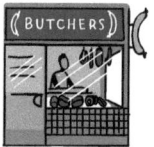

Slachterie

mesnica

BAKERY

Bäckerie

pekara

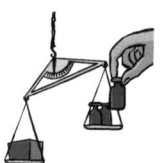

wegen

vagati

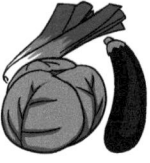

Gröönsaken

povrće

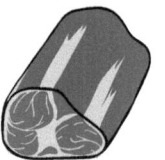

Fleesch

meso

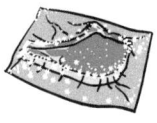

Deepköhlkost

smrznuta hrana

Opsnitt

narezak

Konserven

konzerve

Waschmiddel

sredstvo za pranje

Snoopkraam

slatkiši

Huushooltssaken

artikli za domaćinstvo

Reinmaaktüüch

sredstva za čišćenje

Verköpersche

prodavačica

Kass

blagajna

Kasserer

blagajnik

Inkoopslist

lista za kupovinu

Opsparrtieden

vreme rada

Breeftasch

novčanik

Kreditkoort

kreditna kartica

Tasch

torba

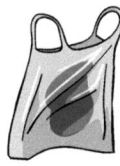

Plastiktüüt

plastična kesa

Water

voda

Saft

sok

Melk

mleko

Cola

kola

Wien

vino

Beer

pivo

Spriet

alkohol

Kakao

kakao

Tee

čaj

Koffie

kava

Espresso

espresso

Cappucino

cappuccino

Banaan

banana

Appel

jabuka

Appelsien

narandža

Meloon

lubenica

Zitroon

limun

Wöttel

šargarepa

Knuuvlook

beli luk

Bambus

bambus

Zibbel

luk

Poggenstohl

gljiva

Nööt

orašasti plodovi

Nudeln

rezanci

Spaghetti

špagete

Ries

riža

Salat

salata

Pommes frites

pomfrit

Braadkantüffeln

pečeni krumpir

Pizza

pica

Hamborger

hamburger

Sandwich

sendvič

Snitzel

šnicla

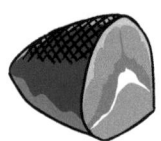

Schinken

šunka

Salami

salama

Wust

kobasica

Hohn

kokoš

Braden

pečenje

Fisch

riba

Eten - jelo

Haverflocken

zobene pahuljice

Müsli

musli

Cornflakes

kukuruzne pahuljice

Mehl

brašno

Croissant

kroasan

Rundstück

pecivo

Broot

hleb

Toast

toast

Keksen

keksi

Botter

maslac

Quark

sveži sir

Koken

kolač

Ei

jaje

Spegelei

jaje na oko

Kees

sir

les
sladoled

Zucker
šećer

Honnig
med

Marmelaad
marmelada

Nougat-Creme
nugat krema

Curry
kari

Buernhoff
seosko gazdinstvo

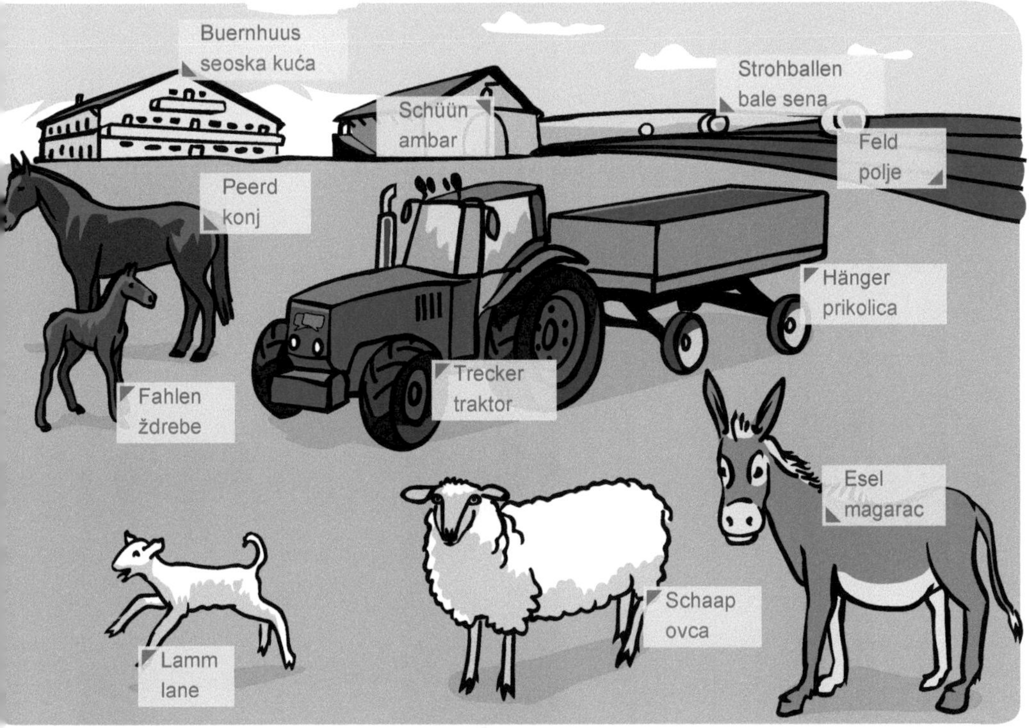

Buernhuus
seoska kuća
Schüün
ambar
Strohballen
bale sena
Feld
polje
Peerd
konj
Hänger
prikolica
Trecker
traktor
Fahlen
ždrebe
Esel
magarac
Schaap
ovca
Lamm
lane

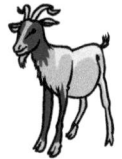

Zeeg
koza

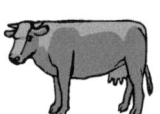

Koh
krava

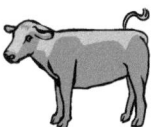

Kalf
tele

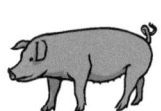

Swien
svinja

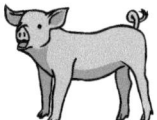

Farken
prase

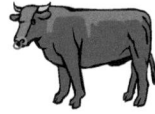

Bull
bik

Goos

guska

Aant

patka

Küken

pilići

Hohn

kokoš

Hahn

petao

Rott

pacov

Katt

mačka

Muus

miš

Oss

vol

Hund

pas

Hunnenhütt

kućica za psa

Goornslauch

vrtno crevo

Geetkann

kanta za polivanje

Lee

kosa

Ploog

plug

Sich

srp

Hack

motika

Mestfork

viljuška za đubrivo

Ext

sekira

Schuufkoor

tačke

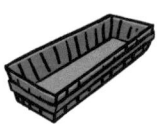

Trog

korito

Melkkann

posuda za mleko

Sack

vreća

Tuun

ograda

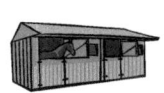

Stall

štala

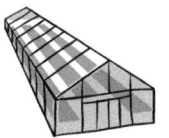

Drievhuus

staklenik

Bodden

zemlja

Saat

seme

Dünger

đubrivo

Meihdöscher

kombajn

oornen

žeti

Oorn

žetva

Yamswöttel

jams začin

Weten

pšenica

Soja

soja

Kantüffel

krumpir

Törksche Weten

kukuruz

Rapp

uljana repica

Aaftboom

voćka

Troopsch Kantüffel

gomolj manioke

Koorn

žitarice

Huus
kuća

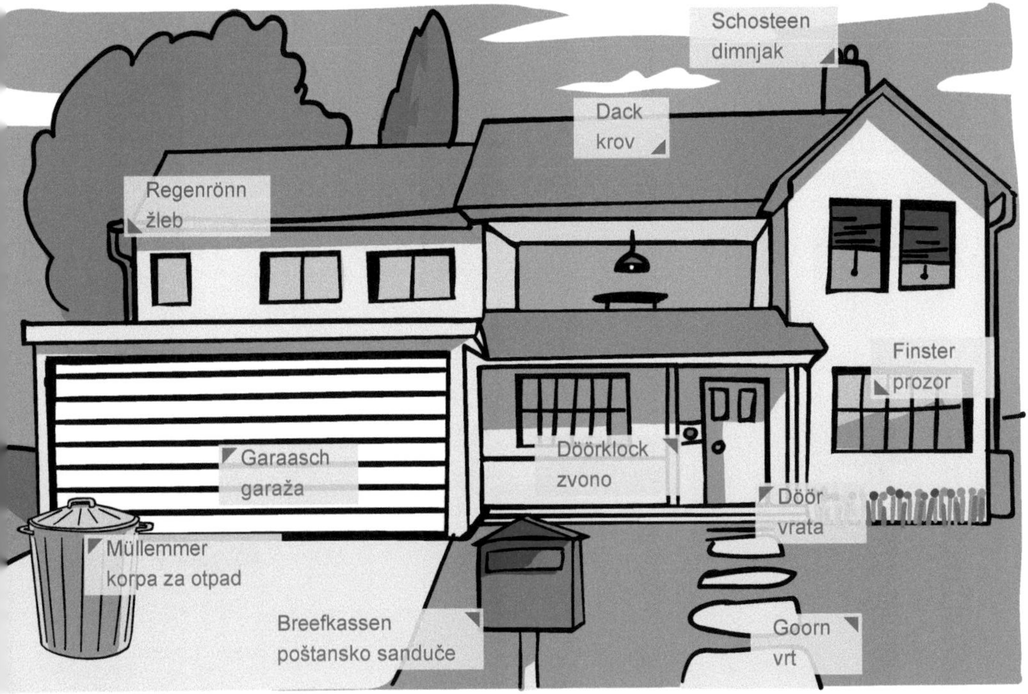
Schosteen
dimnjak
Dack
krov
Regenrönn
žleb
Finster
prozor
Garaasch
garaža
Döörklock
zvono
Döör
vrata
Müllemmer
korpa za otpad
Breefkassen
poštansko sanduče
Goorn
vrt

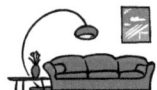

Wahnstuuv
dnevna soba

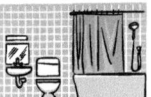

Baadstuuv
kupaonica

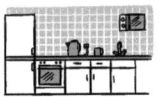

Köök
kuhinja

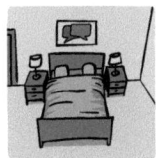

Slaapstuuv
spavaća soba

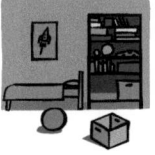

Kinnerstuuv
dečija soba

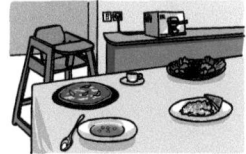

Eetstuuv
trpezarija

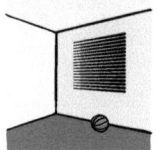

Footbodden

pod

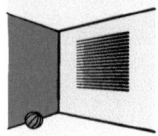

Wand

zid

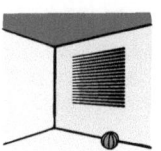

Deek

strop

Keller

podrum

Hittluftbad

sauna

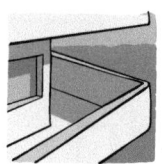

Balkon

balkon

Terrass

terasa

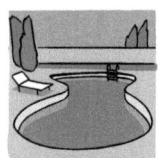

Swümmbad

bazen

Rasenmeiher

kosilica za travu

Bettbetog

posteljina za krevet

Bettdeek

deka za krevet

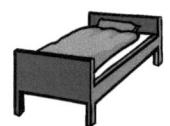

Puuch

krevet

Bessen

metla

Emmer

kanta

Schalter

prekidač

Wahnstuuv

dnevna soba

Tapeet
tapeta
Bild
slika
Lamp
svetiljka
Regal
regal
Schapp
ormar
Kiekkassen
televizija
Kamin
kamin
Bloom
cvijet
Küssen
jastuk
Sofa
kauč
Vaas
vaza
Feernbedenen
daljinski upravljač

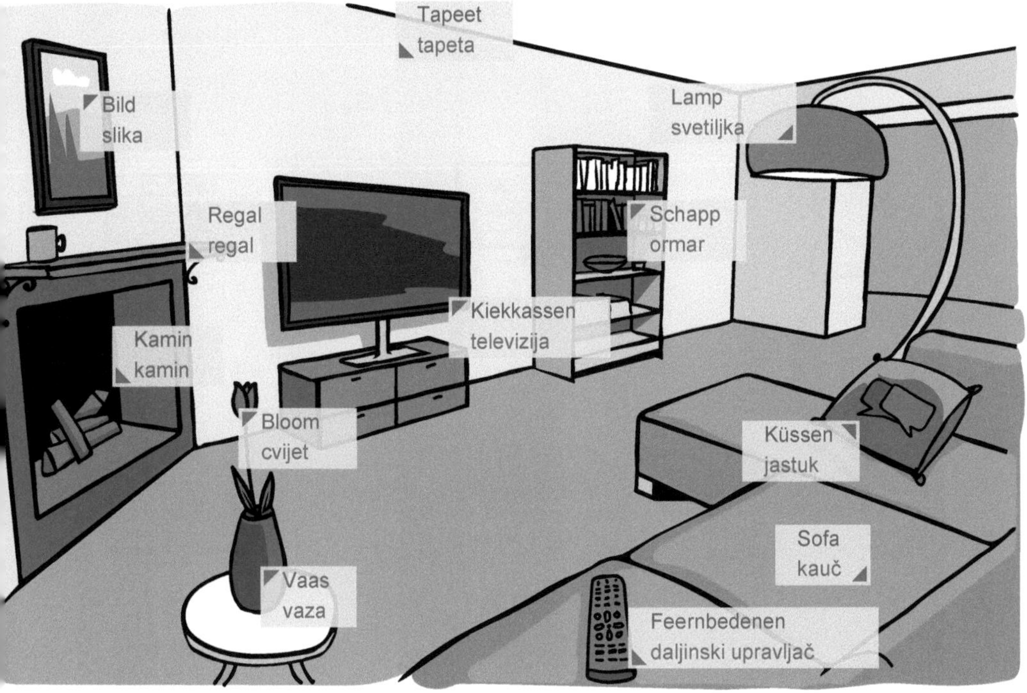

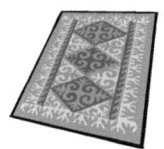

Teppich

tepih

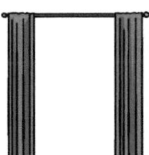

Vörhang

zavesa

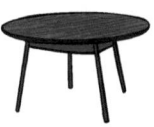

Disch

sto

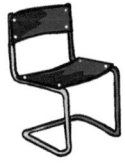

Stohl

stolica

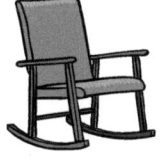

Schuckelstohl

stolica za njihanje

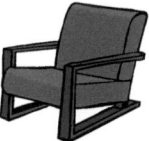

Sessel

fotelja

Book

knjiga

Deek

deka

Dekoratschoon

dekoracija

Füerholt

drvo za ogrev

Film

film

Stereoanlaag

hi-fi uređaj

Slötel

ključ

Narichtenblatt

novine

Gemälde

slika na platnu

Poster

poster

Radio

radio

Opschrievblock

blok za pisanje

Huulbessen

usisivač

Kaktus

kaktus

Kars

sveća

Köök
kuhinja

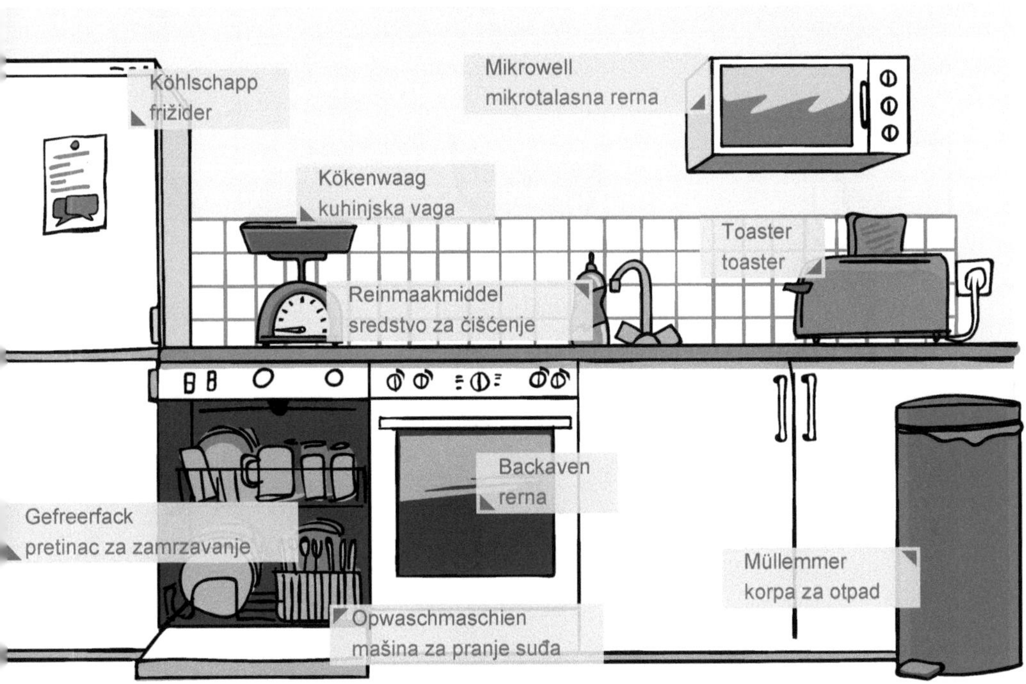

Köhlschapp
frižider
Mikrowell
mikrotalasna rerna
Kökenwaag
kuhinjska vaga
Toaster
toaster
Reinmaakmiddel
sredstvo za čišćenje
Backaven
rerna
Gefreerfack
pretinac za zamrzavanje
Müllemmer
korpa za otpad
Opwaschmaschien
mašina za pranje suđa

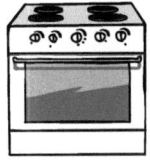

Heerd

šporet

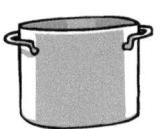

Pott

lonac

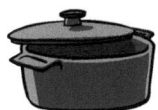

Gussiesern Putt

gvozdeni lonac

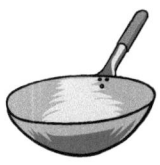

Wok / Kadai

wok / kadai

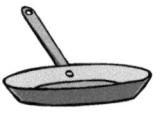

Pann

tava

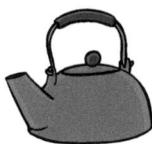

Waterkaker

kuvalo za vodu

Dampkaakputt

kuvalo na paru

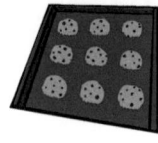

Backblick

lim za pečenje

Geschirr

posuđe

Beker

čaša

Schaal

posuda

Eetsticken

štapići za jelo

Suppenkell

kutlača

Pannenwenner

lopatica

Sneebessen

penjača

Kaakseef

sito za kuvanje

Seef

sito

Riev

ribež

Mörser

mužar

Grill

roštilj

Füerstell

ognjište

Sniedbrett

daska

Nudelholt

oklagija

Proppentrecker

vadičep

Doos

konzerva

Dosenaapner

otvarač konzervi

Pottlappen

krpa za lonac

Waschbecken

sudoper

Böst

četka

Swamm

sunđer

Mixer

mikser

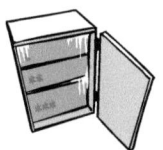

Iesschapp

zamrzivač

Nuckelbuddel

flašica za bebe

Waterhahn

slavina za vodu

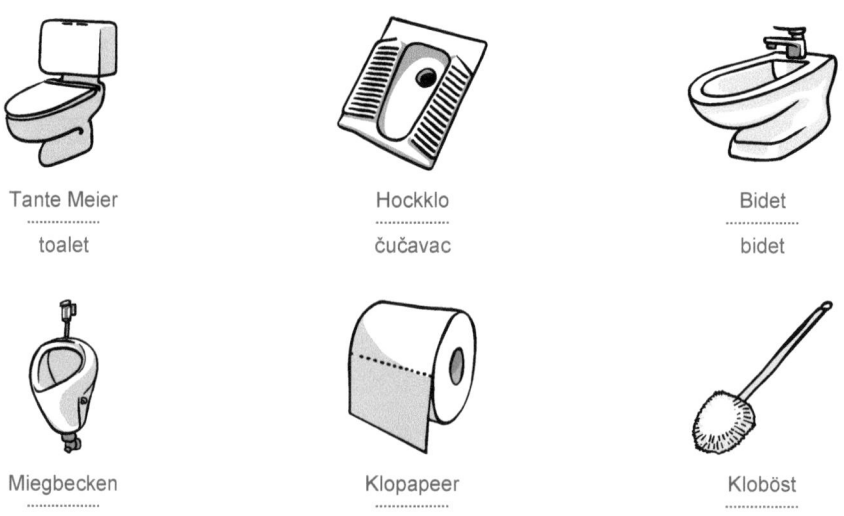

Baadstuuv
kupaonica

Heizung
grejanje
Handdook
peškir
Bruus
tuš
Bruusvörhang
zavesa za tuš
Schuumbad
penušava kupka
Baadwann
kada
Glas
čaša
Waschmaschien
mašina za pranje veša
Waterhahn
slavina za vodu
Fliesen
pločice
lütte Putt
tuta
Waschbecken
sudoper

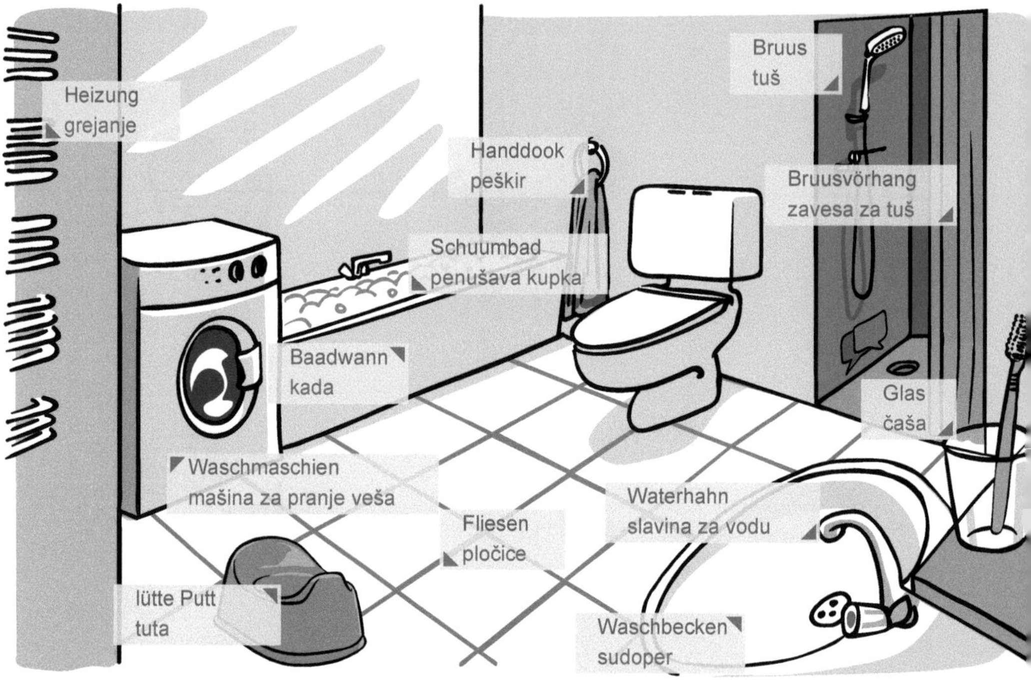

Tante Meier
toalet

Hockklo
čučavac

Bidet
bidet

Miegbecken
pisoar

Klopapeer
toaletni papir

Klobööst
četka za toalet

Tähnböst

četkica za zube

Tähnpast

pasta za zube

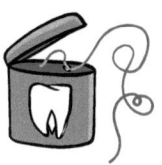

Tähnsied

konac za zube

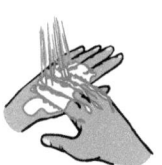

waschen

prati

Handbruus

tuš ručica

Intimbruus

tuš za pranje intimnih
delova

Waschschöttel

lavor

Rüchböst

četka za pranje leđa

Seep

sapun

Bruusgeel

gel za tuširanje

Hoorwaschmiddel

šampon

Waschlappen

krpa za pranje

Afloop

odvod

Creme

krema

Deodorant

dezodorans

Spegel

ogledalo

Kosmetikspegel

kozmetičko ogledalo

Raserer

brijač

Raseerschuum

pena za brijanje

Raseerwater

losion za posle brijanja

Kamm

češalj

Böst

četka

Hoordröger

fen za kosu

Hoorspray

sprej za kosu

Smink

makeup

Lippensticken

ruž za usne

Nagellack

lak za nokte

Watt

vata

Nagelscheer

makaze za nokte

Rüükwater

parfem

Kulturbüdel

kozmetička torbica

Schemel

stolica

Waag

vaga

Baadmantel

ogrtač

Gummihanschen

rukavice za čišćenje

Tampon

tampon

Damenbinn

uložak

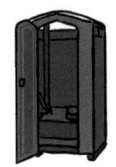

Chemieklo

hemijski toalet

Kinnerstuuv
dečija soba

Wecker
budilnik
Knudeldeert
plišana igračka
Speeltüüchauto
auto igračka
Klöter
zvečka
Poppenhuus
kućica za lutke
Geschenk
poklon

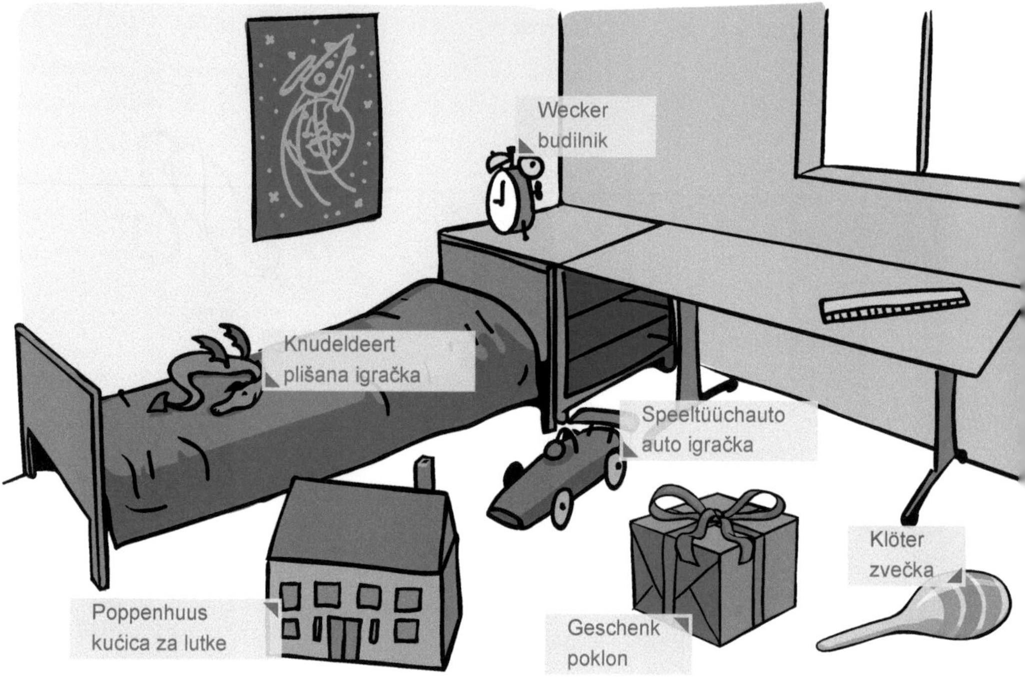

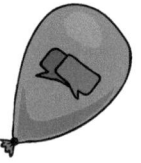

Luftballon

balon

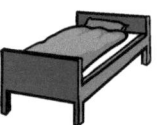

Puuch

krevet

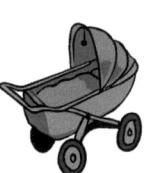

Kinnerwagen

dječija kolica

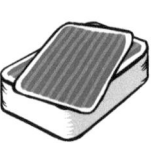

Koortenspeel

igra s kartama

Puzzle

slagalica

SUPER
MEGA

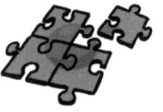

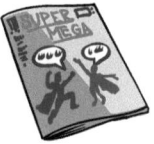

Billergeschicht

strip

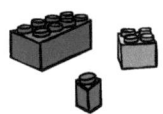

Legostenen

lego kockice

Bustenen

kockice za slaganje

Action-Figur

akcioni junak

Strampelantog

benkica za bebe

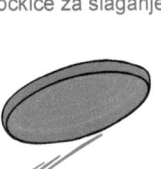

Frisbeeschiev

frizbi

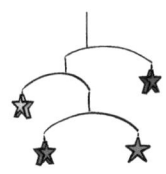

Mobile

viseće igračke

Brettspeel

društvene igre

Wörpel

kocka

Modelliesenbahn

minijaturna željeznica

Snuller

duda

Party

zabava

Billerbook

slikovnica

Ball

lopta

Popp

lutka

spelen

igrati

Sandkassen

pješčanik

Schuckel

ljuljačka

Speeltüüch

igračka

Speelkonsool

konzola za igre

Dreerad

tricikl

Teddyboor

tedi

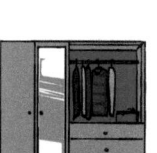

Klederschapp

ormar

Tüüch

odeća

Socken

kratke čarape

Strümp

čarape

Strumpbüx

hulahopke

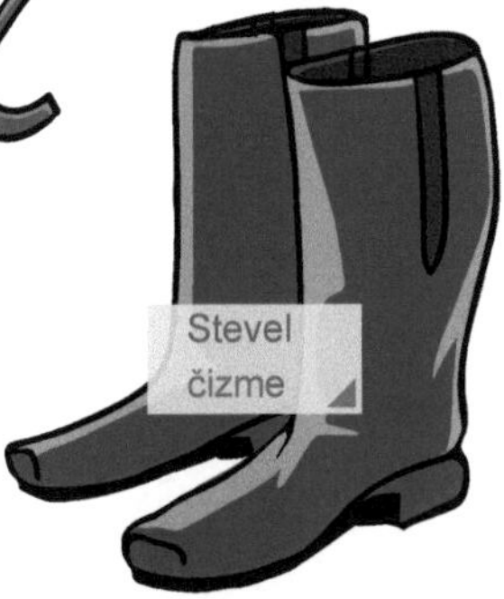

Halsdook
šal

Paraplü
kišobran

T-Shirt
majica

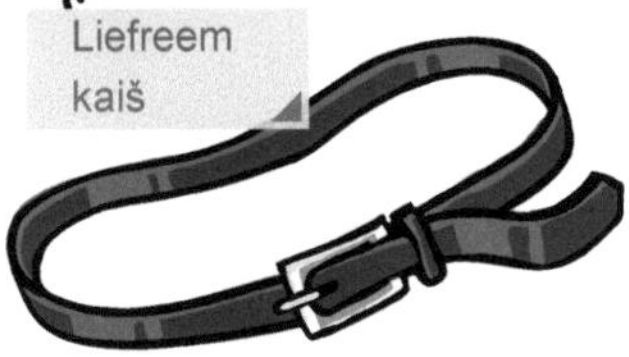

Liefreem
kaiš

Stevel
čizme

Puuschen
papuče

Turnschoh
patike

Sandalen
....
sandale

Schoh
....
cipele

Gummistevel
....
gumene čizme

Ünnerbüx
....
gaćice

Bostholler
....
grudnjak

Ünnerhemd
....
potkošulja

Lief

bodi

Büx

pantalone

Jeansnüx

farmerke

Rock

suknja

Bluus

bluza

Hemd

košulja

Pullover

džemper

Kapuzenpullover

džemper s kapuljačom

Blazer

sako

Jack

jakna

Mantel

kaput

Övertrecker

kabanica

Kostüm

kostim

Kleed

haljina

Hochtietskleed

venčanica

Antog

odelo

Nachtkleed

spavaćica

Slaapantog

pidžama

Sari

sari

Koppdook

marama za glavu

Turban

turban

Burka

burka

Kaftan

kaftan

Abaya

abaja

Baadantog

kupaći kostim

Baadbüx

kupaće gaćice

Korte Büx

kratke pantalone

Antog to'n Öven

odeća za trening

Schört

kecelja

Handschoh

rukavice

Knopp

dugme

Brill

naočare

Armband

narukvica

Halskeed

ogrlica

Ring

prsten

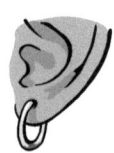

Ohrbummel

naušnica

Mütz

kapa

Klederbögel

vešalica

Hoot

šešir

Binner

kravata

Rietslüter

patent zatvarač

Helm

kaciga

Drachtband

naramenice

Schooluniform

školska uniforma

Uniform

uniforma

Severböten
....
podbradak

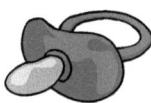

Snuller
....
duda

Winnel
....
pelena

Büro
kancelarija

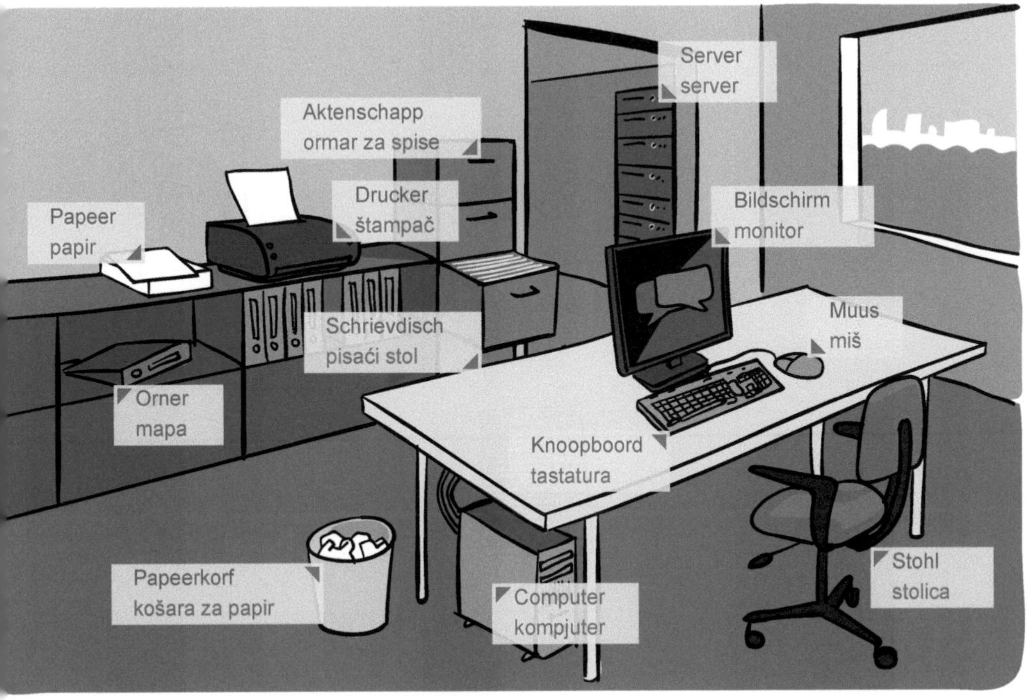

Server
server

Aktenschapp
ormar za spise

Drucker
štampač

Bildschirm
monitor

Papeer
papir

Schrievdisch
pisaći stol

Muus
miš

Orner
mapa

Knoopboord
tastatura

Papeerkorf
košara za papir

Stohl
stolica

Computer
kompjuter

Koffiebeker
....
šalica za kavu

Taschenreekner
....
kalkulator

Internet
....
internet

Klappreekner

laptop

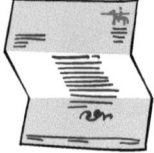

Breef

pismo

Naricht

poruka

Ackersnacker

mobilni telefon

Nettwark

mreža

Kopeerapparat

uređaj za kopiranje

Software

softver

Klöönkassen

telefon

Steekdoos

utičnica

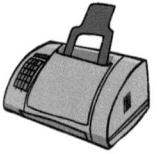

Faxapparat

faks

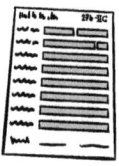

Formulor

formular

Dokument

dokument

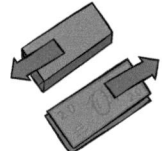

köpen

kupovati

betahlen

platiti

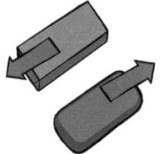

hanneln

trgovati

Geld

novac

USD

Dollar

dolar

EUR

Euro

evro

JPY

Yen

jen

RUB

Ruvel

rublja

CHF

Swiezer Franken

švajcarski franak

CNY

Renminbi Yuan

renmindbi juan

INR

Rupie

rupija

Geldautomat

automat za novac

Wesselstuuv

menjačnica

Gold

zlato

Sülver

srebro

Ööl

nafta

Energie

energija

Pries

cena

Verdrag

ugovor

Stüer

porez

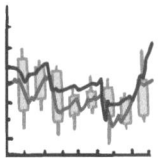

Andeelschien

deonica

arbeiden

raditi

Anstellte

službenik

Arbeitgever

poslodavac

Fabrik

fabrika

Hökerie

prodavnica

Profeschonen
zanimanja

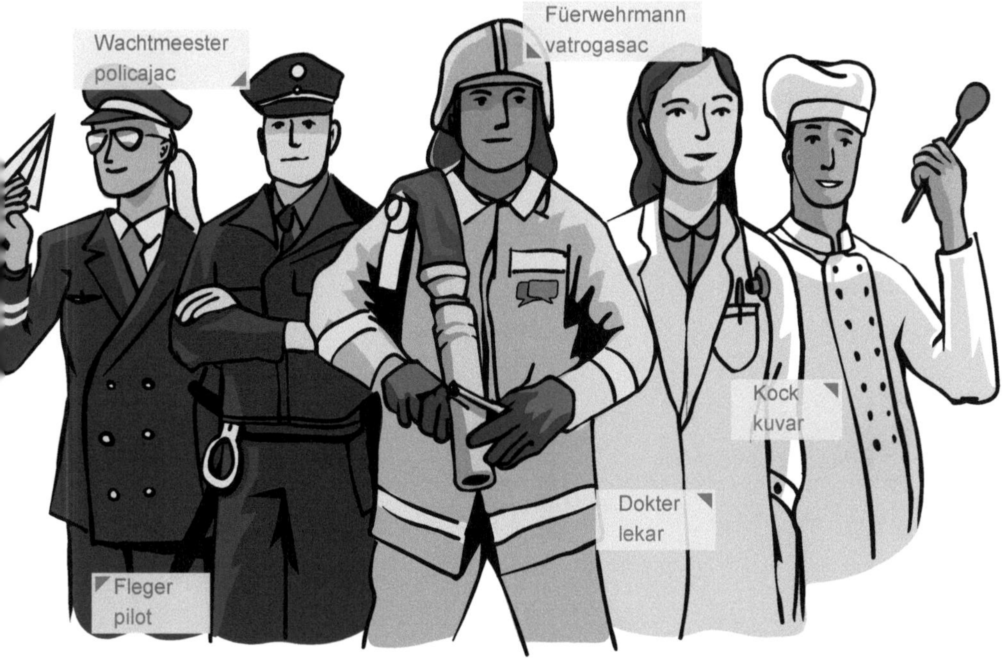

Wachtmeester
policajac
Füerwehrmann
vatrogasac
Kock
kuvar
Dokter
lekar
Fleger
pilot

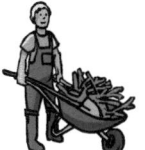

Goorner

vrtlar

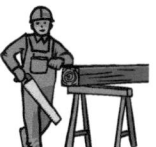

Discher

stolar

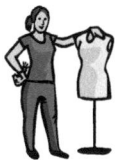

Neihersche

krojačica

Richter

sudija

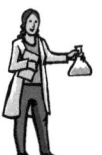

Chemiker

hemičar

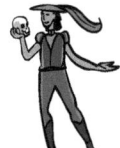

Schauspeler

glumac

Busfohrer	Taxifohrer	Fischer
vozač autobusa	vozač taksija	ribar

Reinmaakfru	Dackdecker	Kellner
čistačica	krovopokrivač	konobar

Jäger	Maler	Bäcker
lovac	slikar	pekar

Elektriker	Buarbeider	Ingenieur
električar	građevinski radnik	inženjer

Slachter	Klempner	Postbüdel
mesar	limar	poštar

Suldat

vojnik

Architekt

arhitekta

Kasserer

blagajnik

Florist

cvećar

Putzbüdel

frizer

Schaffner

kondukter

Mechaniker

mehaničar

Kaptein

kapetan

Tähndokter

zubar

Wetenschopler

naučnik

Rabbi

rabi

Imam

imam

Mönk

monah

Paap

svećenik

Warktüüch

alati

Hamer
čekić
Tang
klešta
Schruvendreiher
odvijač
Schruvenslötel
ključ za zavrtnje
Taschenlamp
džepna lampa

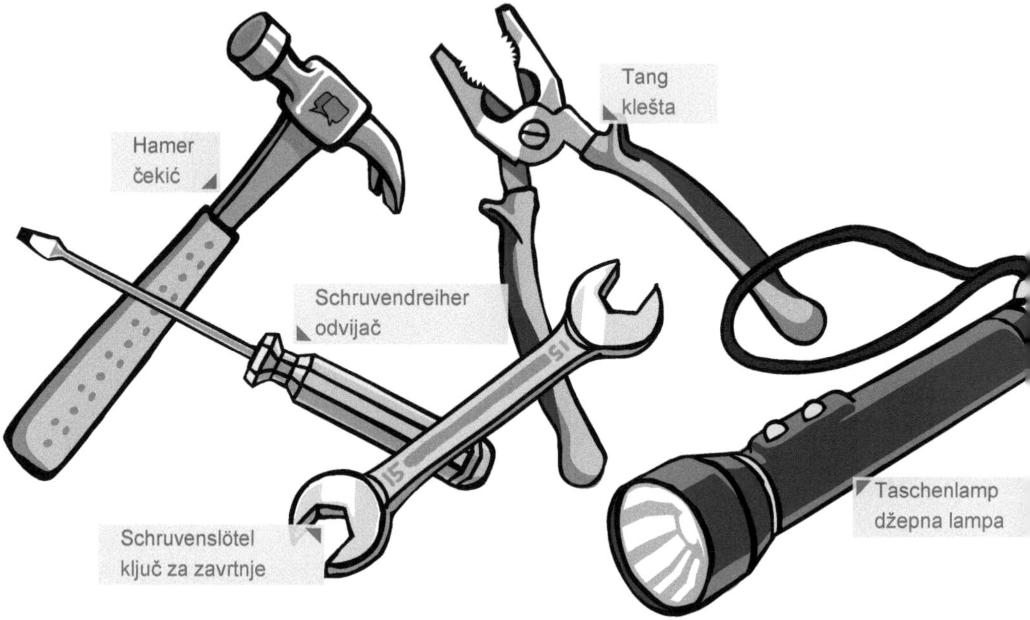

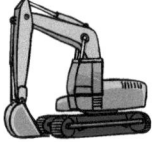

Grieper

bager

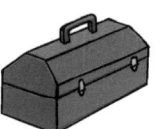

Warktüüchkassen

kutija za alat

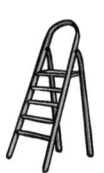

Ledder

merdevine

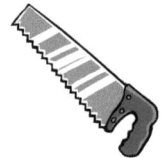

Saag

pila

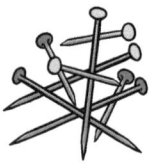

Nagels

ekser

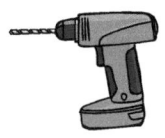

Bohrer

bušilica

heelmaken
popraviti

Schüffel
lopata

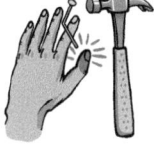

Schiet!
do đavola!

Kehrblick
lopatica

Farvpott
lonac za boju

Schruven
zavrtanji

Musikinstrumenten
muzički instrument

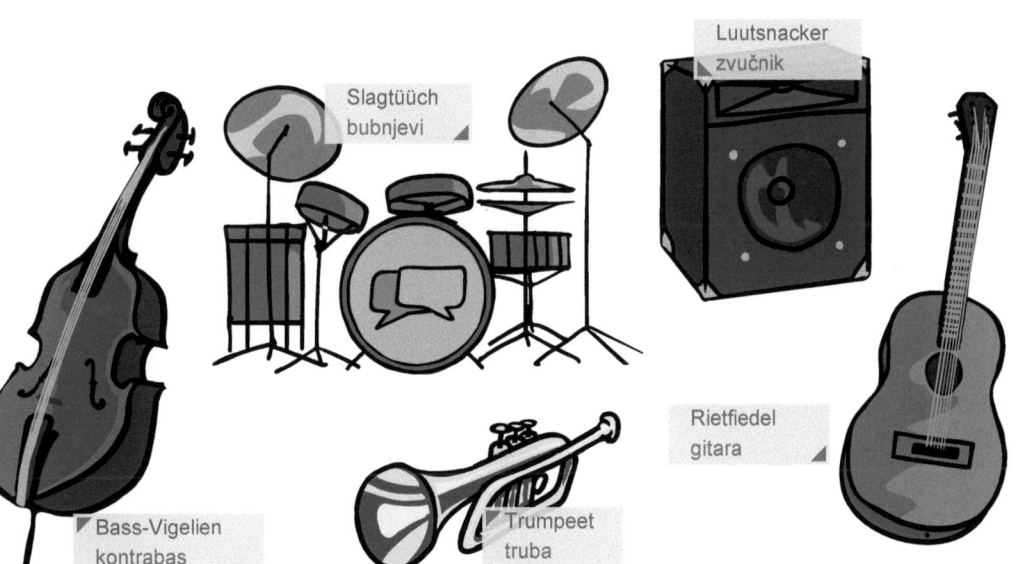

Slagtüüch
bubnjevi

Luutsnacker
zvučnik

Rietfiedel
gitara

Bass-Vigelien
kontrabas

Trumpeet
truba

Klaveer

klavir

Vigelien

violina

Bass

bas

Pauk

timpani

Trummeln

udaraljke za bubnjeve

Keyboard

tipke klavira

Saxophon

saksofon

Fleut

flauta

Mikrofoon

mikrofon

Deertenpark
zoološki vrt

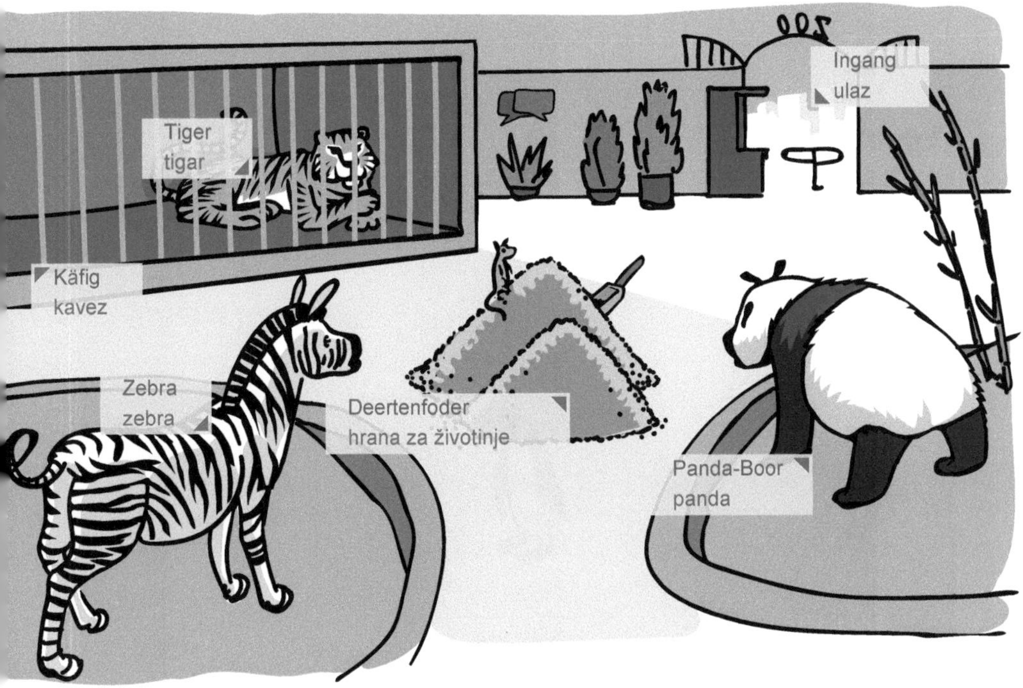

Tiger
tigar
Ingang
ulaz
Käfig
kavez
Zebra
zebra
Deertenfoder
hrana za životinje
Panda-Boor
panda

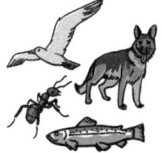

Deerten
životinje

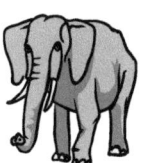

Elefant
slon

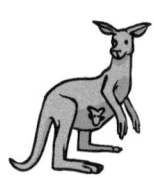

Känguru
kengur

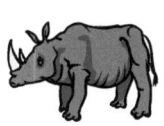

Neeshoorn
nosorog

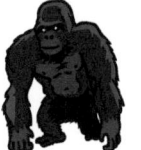

Gorilla
gorila

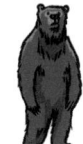

Boor
medved

Kameel

kamila

Struuß

noj

Lööv

lav

Aap

majmun

Flamingo

flamingo

Papagoi

papagaj

Iesboor

polarni medved

Pinguin

pingvin

Haifisch

ajkula

Pageluun

paun

Slang

zmija

Krokodil

krokodil

Oppasser in'n Deertenpark

čuvar u zoološkom vrtu

Saalhund

tuljan

Jaguor

jaguar

Pony

poni

Leopard

leopard

Nilpeerd

nilski konj

Giraff

žirafa

Aadler

orao

Wildswien

divlja svinja

Fisch

riba

Schildkrööt

kornjača

Walross

morž

Voss

lisica

Gazell

gazela

Amerikaansch Football
američki nogomet

Radfohren
biciklizam

Tennis
tenis

Korfball
košarka

Swümmen
plivanje

Boxen
boks

Ieshockey
hokej na ledu

Football
fudbal

Fedderball
badminton

Leichtathletik
atletika

Handball
rukomet

Skilopen
skijanje

Polo
polo

Aktivitäten
aktivnosti

lachen
smejati se
springen
skočiti
ümarmen
zagrliti
gahn
ići
singen
pevati
drömen
sanjati
beden
moliti se
snuteln
poljubiti

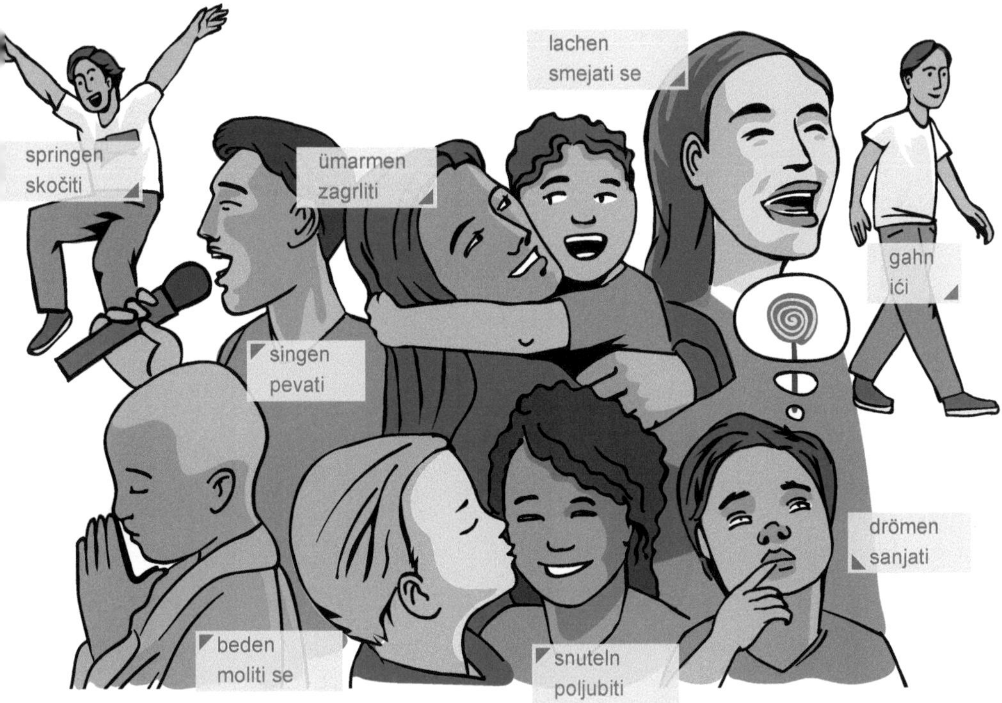

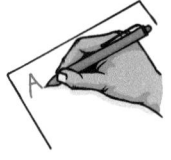

schrieven
pisati

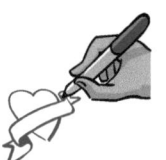

teken
crtati

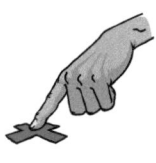

wiesen
pokazati

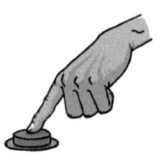

drücken
gurati

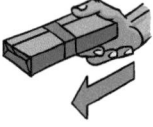

geven
dati

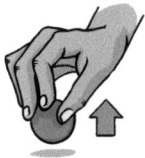

nehmen
uzeti

hebben
imati

doon
činiti

sien
biti

stahn
stojati

lopen
trčati

trecken
povlačiti

smieten
baciti

fallen
padati

liggen
ležati

töven
čekati

dregen
nositi

sitten
sediti

antrecken
oblačiti

slapen
spavati

opwaken
probuditi se

ankieken

gledati

wenen

plakati

eien

milovati

kämmen

češljati

snacken

govoriti

verstahn

razumeti

fragen

pitati

hören

slušati

drinken

piti

eten

jesti

oprümen

pospremiti

leefhebben

voleti

kaken

kuhati

fohren

voziti

flegen

leteti

segeln

ploviti

reken

računati

lesen

čitati

lehren

učiti

arbeiden

raditi

de Plünnen tohoopsmieten

venčati se

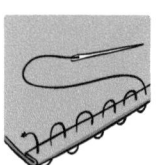

neihen

šiti

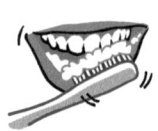

Tähnen putzen

prati zube

dootmaken

ubiti

smöken

pušiti

schicken

poslati

Familje
porodica

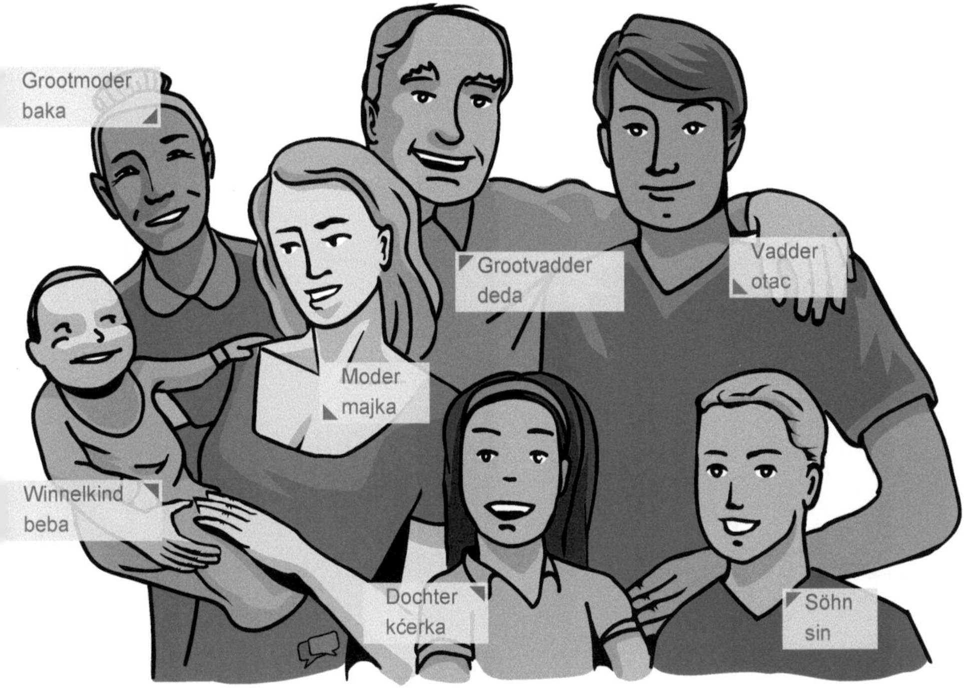

Grootmoder
baka
Grootvadder
deda
Vadder
otac
Moder
majka
Winnelkind
beba
Dochter
kćerka
Söhn
sin

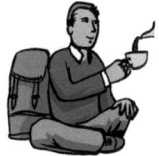

Gast

gost

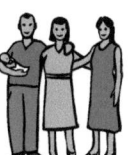

Tant

tetka

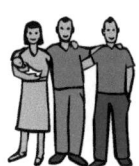

Unkel

ujak, stric

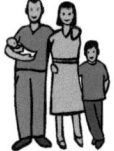

Broder

brat

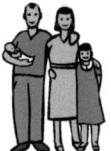

Süster

sestra

Lief
telo

Vörkopp
čelo
Oog
oko
Gesicht
lice
Kinn
brada
Bost
grudi
Finger
prst
Hand
ruka
Arm
ruka
Schuller
rame
Been
noga

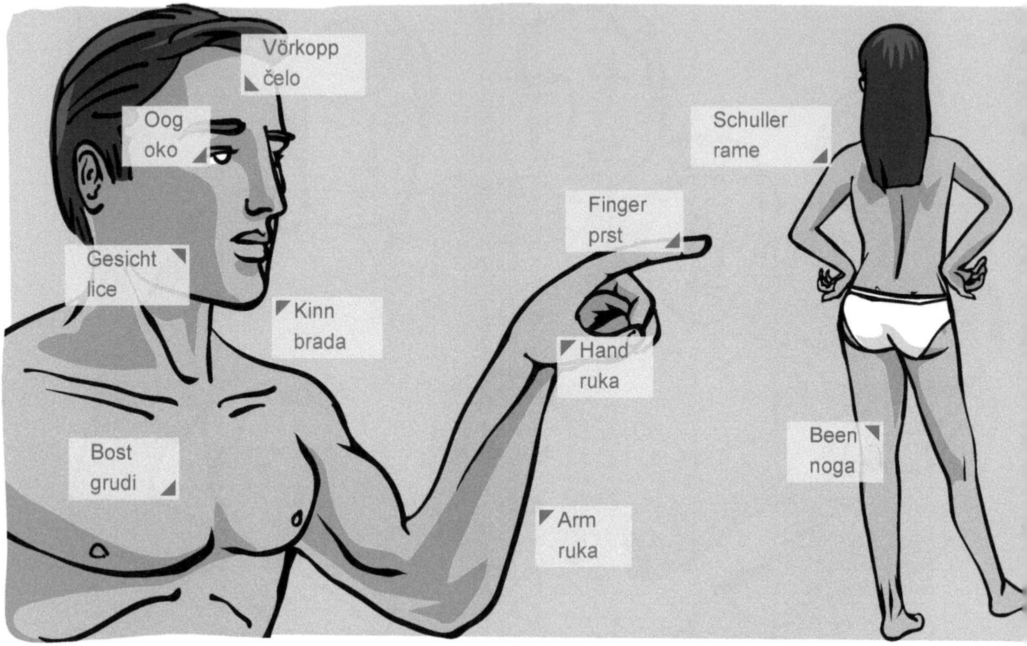

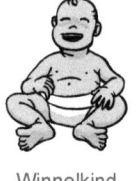

Winnelkind

beba

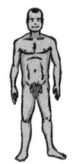

Mann

muškarac

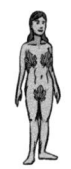

Fro

žena

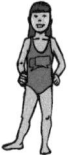

Deern

devojčica

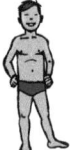

Jung

dečak

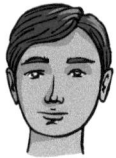

Arm

glava

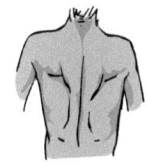

Rüch

leđa

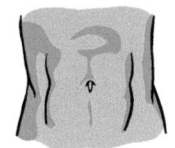

Buuk

stomak

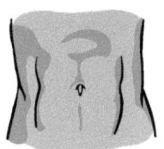

Navel

pupak

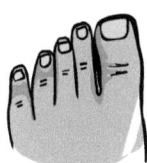

Teh

nožni prst

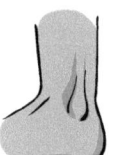

Hack

peta

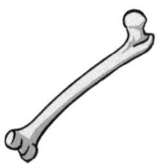

Knaken

kost

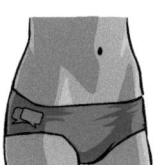

Hüft

kukovi

Knee

koleno

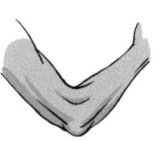

Ellbagen

lakat

Nees

nos

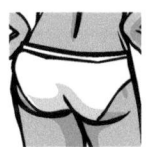

Achtersen

zadnjica

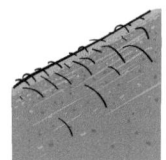

Huut

koža

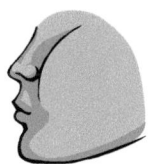

Back

obraz

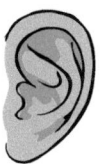

Ohr

uvo

Lipp

usna

Mund

usta

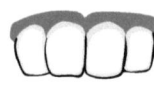

Tähn

zub

Tung

jezik

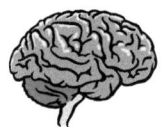

Bregen

mozak

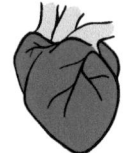

Hart

srce

Muskel

mišić

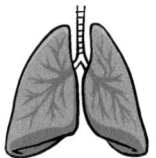

Lung

pluća

Lever

jetra

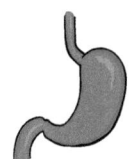

Maag

želudac

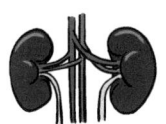

Neren

bubrezi

Bislaap

polni odnos

Kondoom

kondom

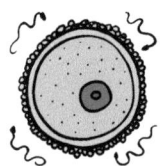

Eizell

jajna ćelija

Sperma

sperma

Anner Ümstänn

trudnoća

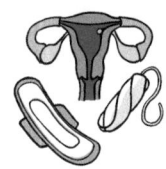

Menstruatschoon

menstruacija

Scheed

vagina

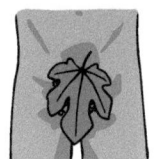

Pint

penis

Ogenbroe

obrva

Hoor

kosa

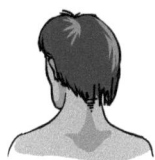

Hals

vrat

Krankenhuus
bolnica

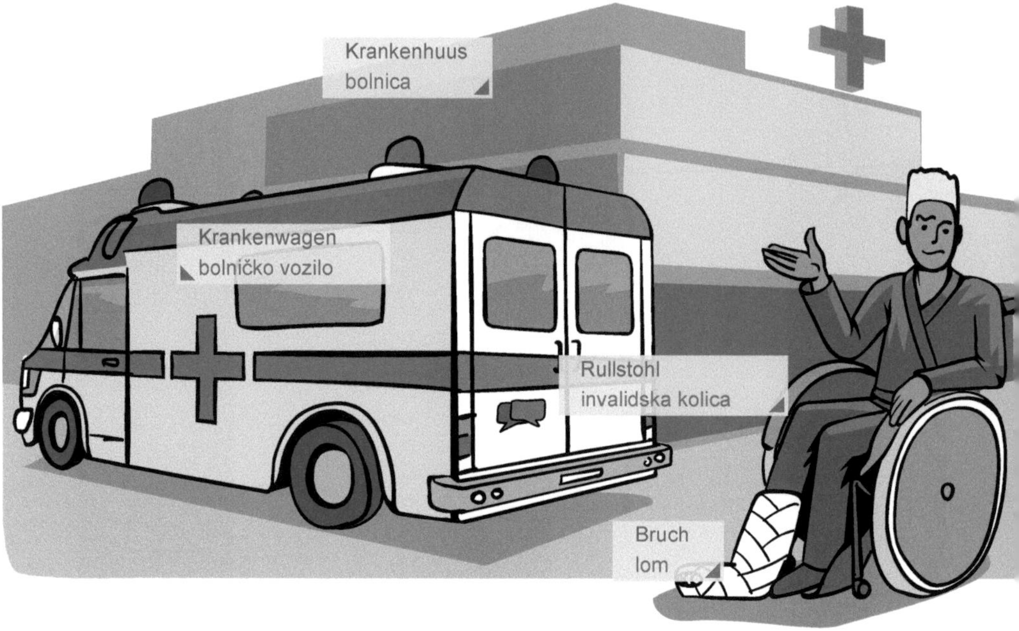

Krankenhuus
bolnica

Krankenwagen
bolníčko vozilo

Rullstohl
invalidska kolica

Bruch
lom

Dokter
lekar

Nootopnahm
hitna medicinska služba

Krankensüster
medicinska sestra

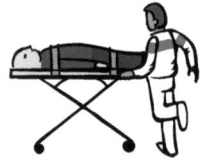

Nootfall
hitni slučaj

ahnmächtig
nesvest

Wehdaag
bol

Verwunnen

povreda

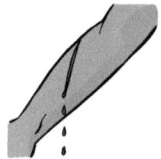

Blöden

krvarenje

Hartinfarkt

srčani udar

Slaganfall

udar

Allergie

alergija

Hoosten

kašalj

Fever

groznica

Gripp

gripa

Dörchfall

proliv

Koppwehdaag

glavobolja

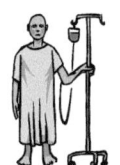

Kreeft

rak

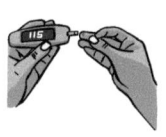

Zuckersüük

dijabetes

Chirurg

hirurg

Chirurgsch Mess

skalpel

Operatschoon

operacija

CT

ct

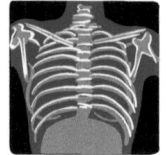

Dörchlüchten

rentgen

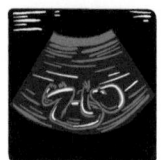

Ultraschall

ultrazvuk

Mask

maska

Krankheit

bolest

Töövruum

čekaona

Krück

štaka

Plaaster

flaster

Verband

zavoj

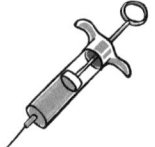

Insprütten

injekcija

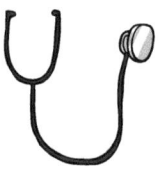

Stethoskop

stetoskop

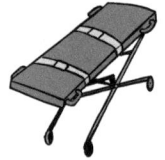

Draag

nosila

Feverthermometer

termometar

Geboort

rođenje

Övergewicht

prekomerna težina

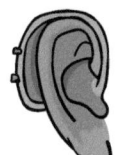

Höörapparat

slušni aparat

Kiemfriemiddel

sredstvo za dezinfekciju

Ansteken

infekcija

Virus

virus

HIV / AIDS

HIV / AIDS

Heelmiddel

medicina

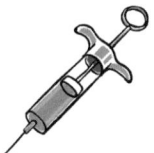

Impen

vakcinacija

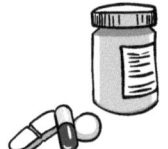

Tabletten

tablete

Pill

pilula

Nootroop

hitni poziv

Blootdruck-Meter

uređaj za merenje pritiska

krank / gesund

bolesno / zdravo

Hölp!

pomoć!

Alarm

alarm

Överfall

nasrtaj

Angreep

napad

Gefohr

opasnost

Nootutgang

izlaz u slučaju nužde

Füer!

požar!

Füerlöscher

protivpožarni aparat

Unfall

nezgoda

Noothölpkoffer

kutija prve pomoći

SOS

sos

Polizei

policija

Europa

Evropa

Noordamerika

Severna Amerika

Süüdamerika

Južna Amerika

Afrika

Afrika

Asien

Azija

Australien

Australija

Atlantik

Atlantik

Pazifik

Pacifik

Indisch Weltmeer

Indijski okean

Antarktisch Weltmeer

Antarktički okean

Arktisch Weltmeer

Arktički ocean

Noordpol

Severni pol

Süüdpol

Južni pol

Antarktis

Antarktik

Eerd

zemlja

Land

zemlja

See

more

Eiland

otok

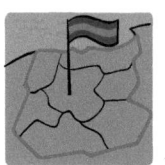

Natschoon

nacija

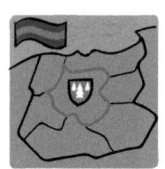

Staat

država

Tallenblatt

brojčanik sata

Stunnenwieser

satna kazaljka

Minutenwieser

minutna kazaljka

Sekunnenwieser

sekundna kazaljka

Wo laat is dat?

Koliko je sati?

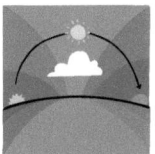

Dag

dan

Tiet

vreme

nu

sada

digetaalsch Klock

digitalni sat

Minuut

minuta

Stunn

čas

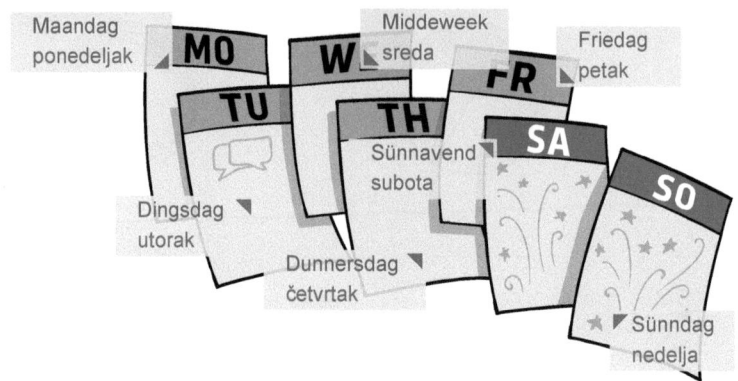

Maandag / ponedeljak
Middeweek / sreda
Friedag / petak
Dingsdag / utorak
Dunnersdag / četvrtak
Sünnavend / subota
Sünndag / nedelja

güstern
juče

hüüt
danas

morgen
sutra

Morgen
jutro

Meddag
podne

Avend
veče

Arbeitsdaag
radni dani

Wekenenn
vikend

Johr
godina

Regen
kiša
Regenbagen
duga
Wind
vetar
Snee
sneg
Fröhjohr
proleće
Harvst
jesen
Sommer
leto
Winter
zima

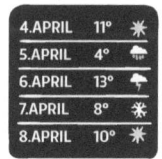

4.APRIL 11°
5.APRIL 4°
6.APRIL 13°
7.APRIL 8°
8.APRIL 10°

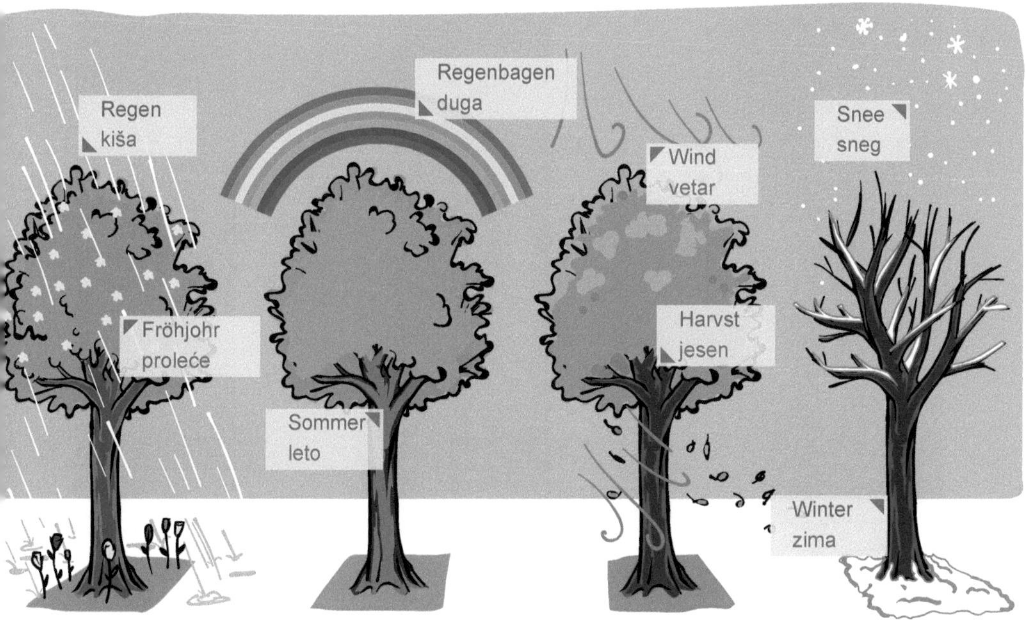

Wedervörhersaag
meteorološka prognoza

F C
120 90 60 30 0 -30
40 30 20 10 0 -10 -20

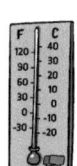

Thermometer
termometar

Sünnenschien
sunčana svetlost

Wulk
oblak

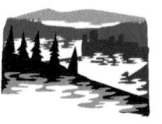

Nevel
magla

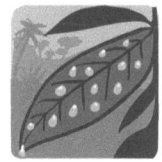

Luftfuchtigkeit
vlažnost vazduha

Blitz

munja

Dunner

grmljavina

Storm

oluja

Hagel

tuča

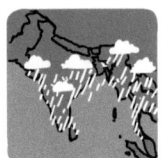

Monsun

monsun

Floot

poplava

Ies

led

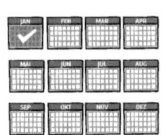

Januormaand

januar

Februormaand

februar

Martmaand

mart

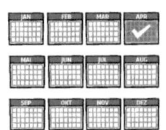

Aprilmaand

april

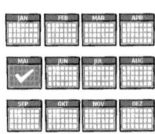

Maimaand

maj

Junimaand

juni

Julimaand

juli

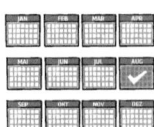

Augustmaand

avgust

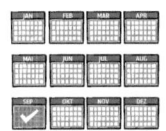

Septembermaand

septembar

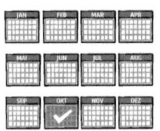

Oktobermaand

oktobar

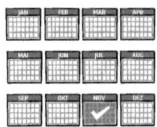

Novembermaand

novembar

Dezembermaand

decembar

Formen
oblici

Krink

krug

Quadrat

kvadrat

Rechteck

pravougao

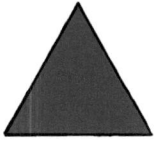

Dreeeck

trougao

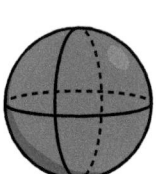

Kugel

kugla

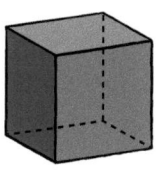

Wörpel

kocka

witt

bela

geel

žuta

orangsch

narandžasta

pink

ružičasta

root

crvena

lila

ljubičasta

blau

plava

gröön

zelena

bruun

smeđa

gries

siva

swart

crna

veel / wenig

mnogo / malo

böös / verdreeglich

ljutito / mirno

smuck / mies

lepo / ružno

Begünn / Enn

početak / kraj

groot / lütt

veliko / maleno

hell / düüster

svetlo / tamno

Broder / Süster

brat / sestra

schier / schietig

čisto / prljavo

kumpleet / nich kumpleet

potpuno / nepotpuno

Dag / Nacht

dan / noć

doot / lebennig

mrtvo / živo

breet / small

široko / usko

geneetbor / nich geneetbor

jestivo / nejestivo

böös / fründlich

zlo / dobro

fickerig / langwielt

uzbuđeno / dosadno

dick / dünn

debelo / mršavo

toeerst / toletzt

na početku / na kraju

Fründ / Fiend

prijatelj / neprijatelj

vull / leddig

puno / prazno

hart / week

tvrdo / mekano

swoor / licht

teško / lagano

Smacht / Döst

glad / žeđ

krank / gesund

bolesno / zdravo

nich na't Recht / na't Recht

ilegalno / legalno

klook / dummerhaftig

pametno / glupo

linkerhand / rechterhand

levo / desno

neeg / feern

blizu / daleko

nieg / bruukt

novo / polovno

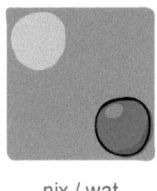

nix / wat

ništa / nešto

oolt / jung

staro / mlado

an / ut

uključeno / isključeno

apen / slaten

otvoreno / zatvoreno

lies / luut

tiho / glasno

riek / arm

bogato / siromašno

richtig / verkehrt

tačno / pogrešno

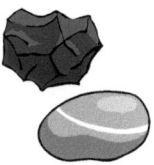

ruug / glatt

hrapavo / glatko

trurig / glücklich

tužno / sretno

kort / lang

kratko / dugo

suutje / flink

polako / brzo

natt / dröög

mokro / suho

warm / köhl

toplo / hladno

Krieg / Freden

rat / mir

0	**1**	**2**
null	een	twee
nula	jedan	dva

3	**4**	**5**
dree	veer	fief
tri	četiri	pet

6	**7**	**8**
söss	söven	acht
šest	sedam	osam

9	**10**	**11**
negen	teihn	ölven
devet	deset	jedanaest

12
twölf
dvanaest

13
dörteihn
trinaest

14
veerteihn
četrnaest

15
föffteihn
petnaest

16
sössteihn
šestnaest

17
söventeihn
sedamnaest

18
achtteihn
osamnaest

19
negenteihn
devetnaest

20
twintig
dvadeset

100
hunnert
stotinu

1.000
dusend
hiljadu

1.000.000
million
milion

Engelsch

engleski

Amerikaansch Engelsch

američki engleski

Chineesch Mandarin

mandarinski kineski

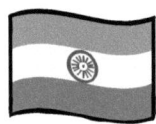

Hindi

hindski

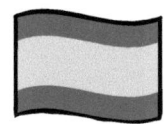

Spaansch

španski

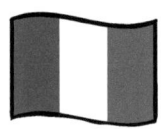

Franzöösch

francuski

Araabsch

arapski

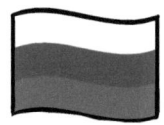

Rusch

ruski

Portugiesch

portugalski

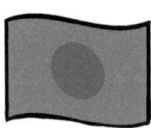

Bengaalsch

bengalski

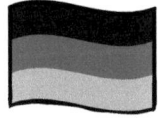

Düütsch

nemački

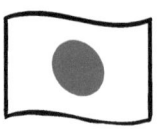

Japaansch

japanski

ik
....
ja

du
....
ti

he / se / dat
....
on / ona / ono

wi
....
mi

ji
....
vi

se
....
oni

keen?
....
Ko?

wat?
....
Šta?

woans?
....
Kako?

woneem?
....
Gde?

wannehr?
....
Kada?

Naam
....
ime

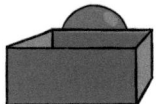

achter

iza

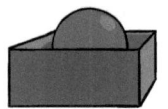

in

u

vör

ispred

över

preko

op

na

ünner

ispod

blangen

pored

twüschen

između

Oort

mesto